NORMAN BRIDWELL

Clifford's®
Big Book of
Things to Know

Cartwheel
·B·O·O·K·S·®

SCHOLASTIC INC.

New York   Toronto   London   Auckland   Sydney   Mexico City   New Delhi   Hong Kong

To those who work so hard to bring reading
to children—the teachers of the world.
—N.B.

Copyright © 1999 by Norman Bridwell.
All rights reserved. Published by Scholastic Inc.
SCHOLASTIC, CARTWHEEL BOOKS and the CARTWHEEL BOOKS logo are trademarks
and/or registered trademarks of Scholastic Inc.
CLIFFORD and CLIFFORD THE BIG RED DOG and associated logos are trademarks
and/or registered trademarks of Norman Bridwell.

Library of Congress Cataloging-in-Publication Data
Bridwell, Norman.
Clifford's big book of things to know / by Norman Bridwell.
        p.   cm.
        Summary: Emily Elizabeth and Clifford share with young readers fun facts they've learned about the human body,
    caring for pets, the seasons, recycling, and much more.
            ISBN 0-590-00385-2
        1. Children's encyclopedias and dictionaries.   [1. Encyclopedias and dictionaries.]
        I. Title.
AG6.875   1999
031.02—DC21   97-45800
                                                                                                      CIP
                                                                                                       AC

12 11 10 9 8 7 6 5 4 3 2 1   9/9 0/0 01 02 03 04

Printed in Singapore   46
First printing, August 1999

Hi! I'm Emily Elizabeth
and this is Clifford, my big red dog.
Clifford and I are very curious.
That means we like to learn
about everything.
In this book, you'll find
out lots of neat things
that Clifford and I have
learned together!

Table of Contents

Your Body, Inside and Out

You can't see what's inside your body. But you can feel some of the things that are inside, like your hard elbow and knee bones. You have bones from your head down to your toes. All of your bones together are called your **skeleton**. The skeleton holds up your body.

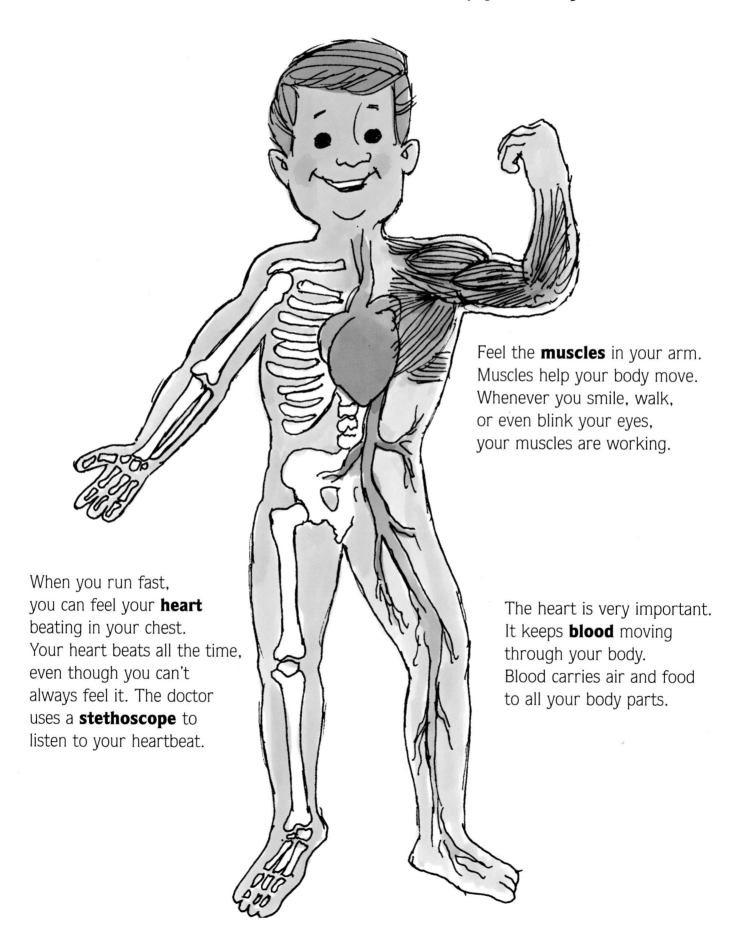

Feel the **muscles** in your arm. Muscles help your body move. Whenever you smile, walk, or even blink your eyes, your muscles are working.

When you run fast, you can feel your **heart** beating in your chest. Your heart beats all the time, even though you can't always feel it. The doctor uses a **stethoscope** to listen to your heartbeat.

The heart is very important. It keeps **blood** moving through your body. Blood carries air and food to all your body parts.

Your body is always
growing and changing.
See how Clifford grew!

newborn

a growing pup

Your body needs
fresh air to breathe,
water to drink,
healthy food to eat,
and a good night's sleep!

MILK

all grown up

ANTI SEPTIC

If you scrape or cut yourself, blood from
inside your body comes out. Wash the
cut with soap and water. Put some first aid cream on the cut to kill
germs and help it heal faster. Cover the cut with a bandage. Soon the
skin will be healed, and you won't even be able to tell you had a cut!

7

Sports and Games

Playing outside is fun, and it's good exercise, too. Running, jumping, and climbing make your muscles strong and keep your heart and lungs healthy. Give your body some exercise every day!

riding

running

sliding

swinging

jumping rope

biking

in-line skating

CLUB HOUSE

climbing

hiking

dancing

BALLET · JAZZ · TAP

GYMNASTICS WORLD

tumbling

diving

swimming

Playing With Balls

Kick the **soccer ball** into the net for a goal.

Hit the **baseball** with the bat and run to first base.

Throw the **basketball** through the hoop to make a shot.

Catch the **football** and run for a touchdown!

9

Growing a Garden

A little **seed** can grow into a big plant. It needs warm weather, sunlight, water, and some soil to dig its roots into. Once you plant a seed, before long, it grows a **stem**, **leaves**, and **flowers**. If the seed comes from a tomato, the plant grows tomatoes. Inside the tomatoes are more seeds.

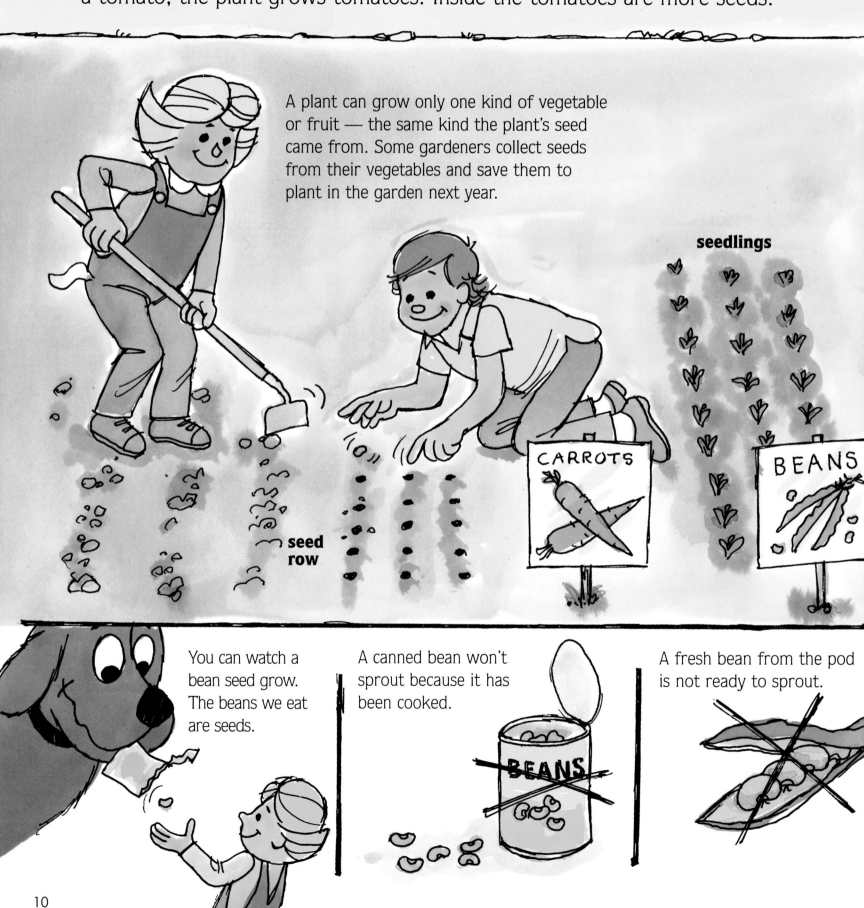

A plant can grow only one kind of vegetable or fruit — the same kind the plant's seed came from. Some gardeners collect seeds from their vegetables and save them to plant in the garden next year.

seedlings

CARROTS

BEANS

seed row

You can watch a bean seed grow. The beans we eat are seeds.

A canned bean won't sprout because it has been cooked.

A fresh bean from the pod is not ready to sprout.

BEANS

10

sunlight

Don't pick the flowers that grow on vegetable plants! Vegetables will grow from the flowers.

water

plants

soil

SQUASH

TOMATOES

A dried bean will sprout! Set the bean on a wet paper towel in a clear plastic cup. Put the cup near a sunny window.

Keep the paper towel wet. After a few days, the bean will sprout. When the little plant begins to make leaves...

seed coat

root

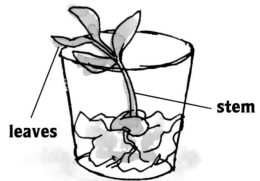

...it will need soil and water. Plant it in a flower pot or outside if the weather is warm.

leaves

stem

11

Taking Care of Pets

Pets are animals that depend on you to take care of them. They need a place of their own where they can rest and feel safe. Some pets stay inside. Some stay outside. Some can go in and out by themselves if you make them a pet door.

All pets need **water** and **food** every day. Each pet needs its own special kind of food.

Pets need **exercise** every day. A hamster gets exercise by running on the wheel in its cage. Bigger pets need outdoor exercise.

Pets need your help to stay clean. Pet owners **wash** and **brush** their animals often. They keep their pets' cages and houses clean.

Pets need **love** and **attention** from their owners.

Having a pet is a big responsibility, but it can be lots of fun!

13

Insects and Spiders

bee

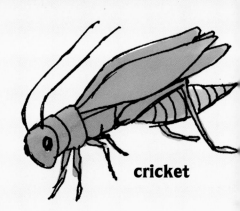

cricket

Most **insects** are small.
Some are *tiny*.
There are more insects in
the world than all the other
animals put together.
Insects have six legs.
A bee, a ladybug, an ant, and
a grasshopper are all insects.

ladybug

ant

Insects have two **antennae**.
The antennae help insects to taste,
touch, hear, and smell the world around them.
Some insects have wings. Male crickets make a
chirping sound by rubbing their wings together.

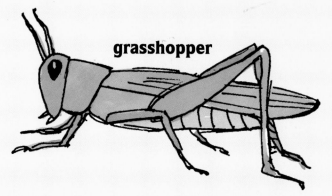

grasshopper

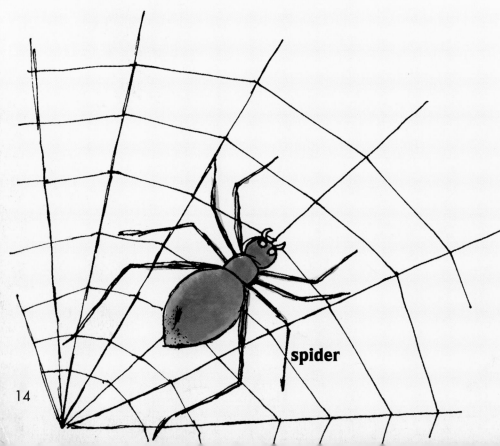

spider

Spiders are not insects.
They are called **arachnids**,
and they have eight legs.
Their bodies make silky threads
that they spin into webs.
A spider's web is a sticky trap!
It catches insects, such as flies,
that the spider needs for food.

14

A moth lays a tiny egg. It's smaller than a grain of rice! When the egg hatches, a tiny **caterpillar** comes out.

It eats leaves...

and sheds its skin...

and grows bigger.

Then the caterpillar spins a **cocoon** around its body. The caterpillar rests inside the cocoon for a long time, while its body changes.

moth

When the cocoon opens, out comes a beautiful moth. It flies away and looks for some flower **nectar** to drink. Later the moth will find a partner. Then it will lay its own tiny eggs.

Animal Homes

Wild animals make homes or sleeping spots where they can be snug and safe. Animal babies are usually born in these safe places. Most animals sleep at night, but some sleep during the day. Raccoons, mice, skunks, and rabbits come out of their homes at night to look for food.

beehive

deer thicket

bear den

rabbit burrow

skunk den

fox hole

doghouse

bird nest

squirrel nest

raccoon den

mouse burrow

beaver lodge

duck nest

The Seasons

spring

summer

Spring is the time of year when the weather turns warmer. Flowers bloom. The trees get new leaves. Farmers plant seeds. Many baby animals are born in spring.

Summer is when days are long and hot. People go swimming and eat ice cream cones to keep cool. On the farm, fields of crops grow higher. At dinner time the sun is still shining. Fireflies come out after dark.

Rain and Snow

When the air is very cold, clouds make **snow** instead of rain. The water droplets inside the clouds freeze into tiny pieces of ice. Some ice crystals grow into **snowflakes**. Every snowflake looks different from the others!

Rain clouds are made of tiny drops of water floating in the air. Every time two water droplets touch, they come together to make a bigger drop of water. If the **raindrops** inside the cloud are too big and heavy to float, they fall out of the cloud, and we say it's raining.

18

autumn

winter

Autumn brings cooler weather. Leaves on the trees turn red, yellow, orange, and brown and fall to the ground. That's why some people call this season "fall." Autumn is the time to harvest corn and wheat, gather nuts, and pick apples and pumpkins.

Winter days are cold and short. It's dark before dinner time. Everyone wears coats to keep warm outside. Sometimes it snows. Groundhogs, bears, and squirrels go into **hibernation**. They stay in their dens and sleep all winter.

Sometimes after it rains there's a **rainbow** in the sky. The air is still very wet. When the sun shines on the water in the air, stripes of colored light appear.

The **sun** is a big ball of burning gases. It makes its own light.

sun

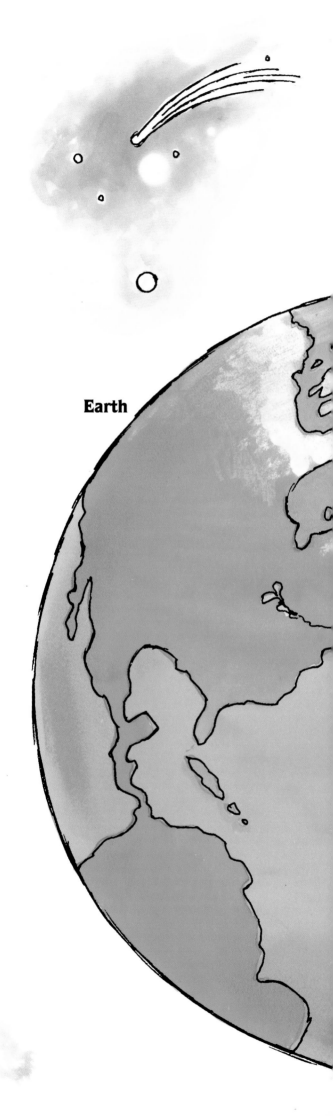

Earth

The **Earth** moves in two ways: it spins, and it also moves around the sun.

The Earth's spinning makes night and day. As the Earth spins, the side that faces the sun has daylight; the side that doesn't face the sun is dark.

The Earth, Sun, and Moon

Your neighborhood is just a small part of the huge, round planet we live on: the planet **Earth**. When we are standing, the earth doesn't seem round. It seems flat. That's because we are very, very small compared to the whole Earth.

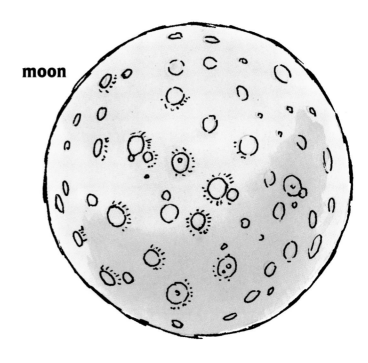

moon

The **moon** doesn't make light. It's just a big rock that moves around the earth. Moonlight is really light from the sun that shines on the moon.

Space

In addition to Earth, there are eight other planets that move around the sun. The nine planets and the sun make up our **solar system**.

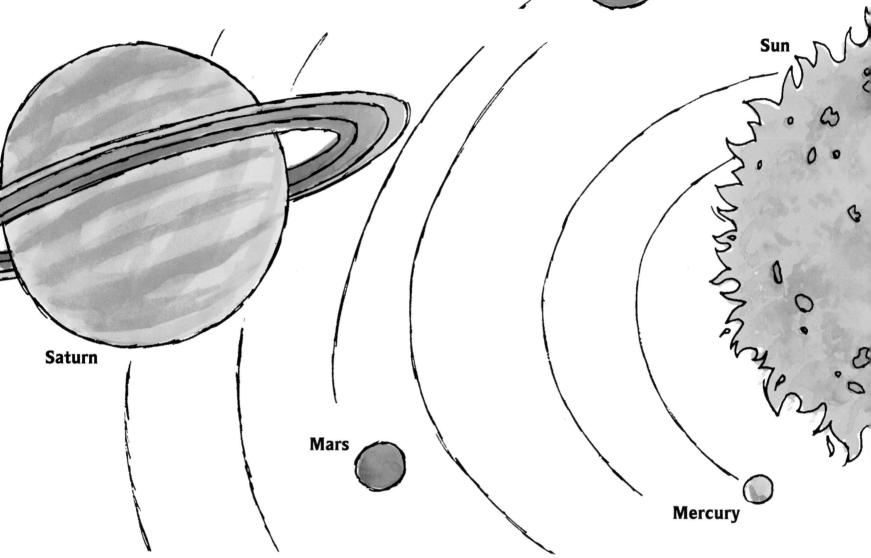

Earth

Sun

Saturn

Mars

Mercury

A Trip on the Space Shuttle

Five, four, three, two, one, zero, lift off!
The **space shuttle** zooms away from the earth, through the clouds, and into space.

The astronauts make a **space walk** to fix a broken **weather satellite**. **Space suits** help them breathe and keep them safe in space.

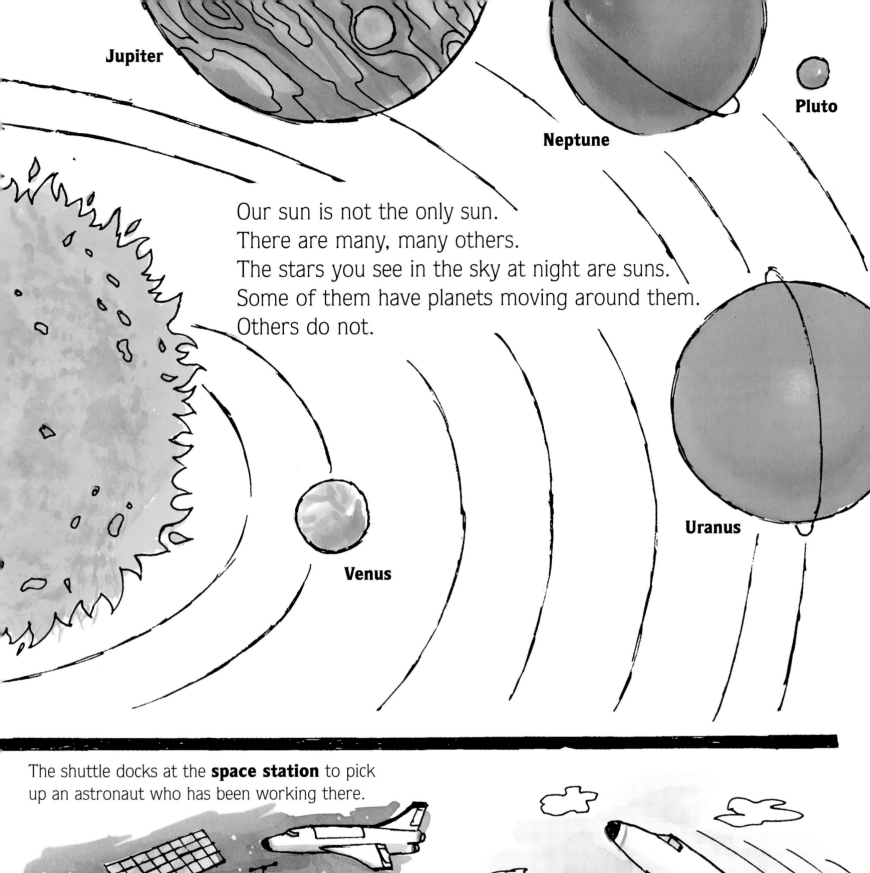

Jupiter

Neptune

Pluto

Our sun is not the only sun.
There are many, many others.
The stars you see in the sky at night are suns.
Some of them have planets moving around them.
Others do not.

Uranus

Venus

The shuttle docks at the **space station** to pick up an astronaut who has been working there.

The space shuttle glides down from the sky and lands on the **runway**. Another successful mission!

23

Clifford's Rock Collection

Rocks come in all shapes and colors!

granite

limestone

quartzite

sandstone

shale

slate

24

Collecting rocks

People who collect rocks are called **rock hounds**. They try to find different kinds of rocks. Not all rocks are hard. Some are soft and crumbly. Some have sparkly mineral bits in them. Most rocks have sharp edges and feel rough, but rocks in a stream can be smooth. That's because water has washed over them for many years and polished away their rough edges.

Small rocks were once huge mountains of rock. As time goes by, wind, rain, and earthquakes break up rocks into smaller and smaller pieces. Soil and sand are made from ground-up rocks.

The objects on the right may look like rocks, but they are not. They were made by people.

brick chip

sidewalk concrete

street pavement

glass

Volcanoes

A **volcano** is a crack in the ground where fiery, melted rock, called **lava**, flows out of the earth.

Great heat and pressure inside the earth can make some volcanoes explode, or **erupt**. Hot ash and lava pour out and cover everything for miles around. Scientists who study volcanoes can usually tell when a dangerous volcano is about to erupt, so people can get away safely.

Most volcanoes, including this underwater volcano, are cone or bowl shaped at the top. Lava flows out and piles up around the opening.

Air or water cools the lava and turns it back into solid rock.

This underwater volcano grows larger each time it erupts.

Finally it becomes an island in the ocean.

The Seashore

Splash! At the shore, ocean **waves** toss seashells onto the beach. The ocean never stops moving. Twice a day it is **high tide**. The ocean water washes high up onto the land and covers most of the beach. Then the tide slowly goes out. At **low tide** the beach is big and wide — perfect for collecting seashells.

sand dune

lobsters

Seashells come from animals. Sea creatures like clams and oysters grow hard shells that protect their soft bodies. Put a seashell to your ear and you may hear a quiet roar. It sounds like the ocean waves!

seaweed

clam

clam shell

sandpiper

sand castle

seagull

Ocean water is not like the water that comes from lakes or rivers. Ocean water is salty. It is not good for drinking. But it makes a good home for many different kinds of plants and animals. Clifford and Emily Elizabeth love the ocean!

dolphin

sand crab

starfish

sand dollar

tide pool

hermit crab

minnows

27

Under the Sea

Under the ocean waves is a colorful world where sharks, sea horses, fish, and other sea creatures live. The floor of the ocean isn't flat like the bottom of a pool. There are mountains and hills on the ocean floor. There are underwater canyons so deep they could hold one of the tallest mountains on earth.

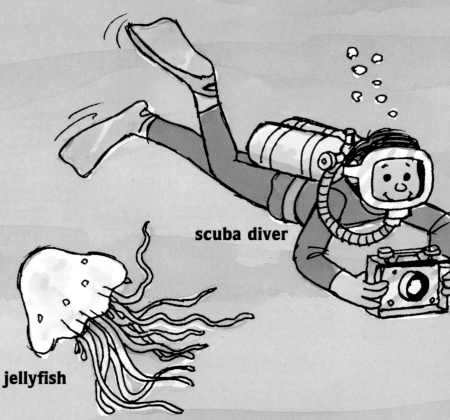

shark

scuba diver

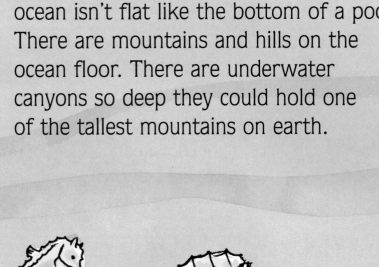

sea horses

jellyfish

People who study sea plants and animals explore the ocean floor in special underwater ships called **submersibles**.

Most of the earth is covered with oceans. A **globe** is a ball-shaped map of the earth. It shows the land and all the oceans.

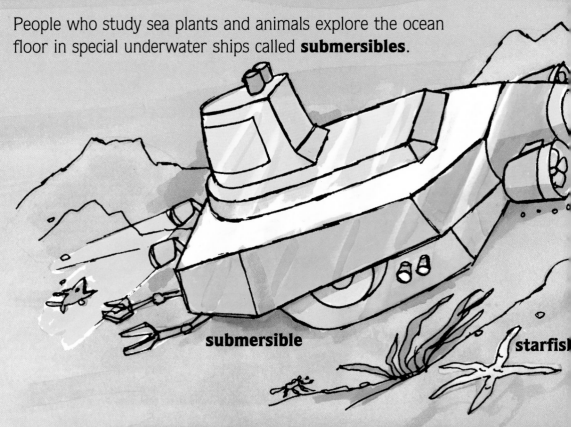

submersible

starfish

whale

People can't breathe underwater. Scuba divers swim with air tanks on their backs. A hose from the air tank to the diver's mouth lets a diver breathe air underwater.

squid

eel

sea turtle

stingray

octopus

seaweed

sunken ship

oysters

lobster

crab

coral

29

Building a House

It takes many people working together to build a new house!

backhoe

A new house begins with drawings known as **blueprints**, that show the size and shape of all the rooms. A **backhoe** digs a hole exactly the right size for the house.

Workers called **masons** pour concret from the **cement mixer** into the hol to make a sturdy **foundation**. The foundation will hold up the house.

cemer mixer

foundation

Plumbers attach new **pipes** to the main water and sewer pipes under the street. The new pipes will carry clean water into the house and dirty water out of the house.

Carpenters put up the wooden **frame**, which is like the skeleton of the house. Then the **walls** and **roof** are put on.

frame

pipes

An **electrician** puts in **wires** and **electrical outlets**. The electrical wires and telephone wires are connected to the **utility pole** on the street.

A **plumber** puts a **furnace** in the cellar to keep the house warm.

Carpenters nail down the floors, put up the inside **walls**, and put in **windows** and **doors**.

Finally, **painters** paint the house, inside and out.

utility pole

window

door

wires

outlet

walls

CLIFFORD

A Recycling Plant

Many families save used plastic bottles, glass jars, metal cans, and newspaper for the **recycling truck**. The recycling truck picks up trash that can be made into something else and used again.

At the recycling center, workers and machines sort and break down each material. Then trucks take the broken-down plastic, glass, metal, and paper to different factories that use recycled materials to make new things.

The recycling truck has separate bins for plastic, metal, glass, and paper.

COUNTY RECYCLING

COUNTY RECYCLING CENTER

PAPER BALER

100% RECYCLED PAPER PRODUCTS

Newspapers are separated from other paper and cardboard. The newspaper is gathered into large stacks. Then it is sent to a paper mill to be made into cardboard **egg cartons**, **game boards**, and more **newspapers**.

Other kinds of paper and cardboard a flattened and stacked. Another factor will make them into new **boxes**.

Metal cans move along a conveyor belt past a large magnet which pulls the steel cans away from the aluminum cans. The steel cans are smashed and chopped into pieces. They are sent to a factory to be melted and made into metal parts for **washing machines** and **refrigerators**.

Aluminum cans are smashed flat and pressed into big blocks. These are sent to a factory where the aluminum will be melted and made into products such as **canoes** and **baseball bats**.

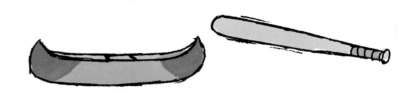

ELECTRO-MAGNET SEPARATING STEEL CANS

ALUMINUM CAN CRUSHER

PLASTIC BOTTLES

VACUUM UNITS

CONVEYOR BELTS

SHREDDER

BLUE GLASS

BROWN GLASS

GREEN GLASS

CLEAR GLASS

BINS

Glass bottles are sorted by color. Then the glass is ground up and sent to a factory. The ground glass will be melted and used to make new glass bottles.

APPLE JUICE

KETCH

MUSTARD

PICKLES

Plastic bottles go down the conveyor belt into a shredding machine and then the chips are cleaned. Next they are sent to a factory where they will be melted. The melted plastic will be poured into molds to make **playground equipment, flowerpots**, and **video cassettes**.

33

Mailing a Letter

Emily Elizabeth is on a trip. She has written a letter to a special friend back home. Emily Elizabeth folds her letter and puts it in an **envelope**.

She writes the **address** on the front of the envelope.

She sticks a **stamp** on the upper right corner.

Then she drops the letter into the **mailbox**.

That night a **mail carrier** opens the mailbox with a key. She puts all the letters into her mailbag. The mail carrier takes all the mail to the **post office**.

At the post office, a machine stamps a **postmark** on each letter. The postmark tells the date and the town where the post office is. Another worker reads the address on every envelope. She puts each letter into a bag with other letters going to the same town.

A truck takes the **mailbags** to the airport. Then a plane carries Emily Elizabeth's letter to her friend's town.

When the plane lands, a mail carrier picks up the **mailbag**. She takes it to the post office.

A worker sorts the mail into the mail carriers' pouches.

The mail carrier takes each letter to the street and house number written on the envelope.

Everyone loves to get a letter in the mail — especially Clifford! 35

Digging a Tunnel

Have you ever wondered how a tunnel is made? A huge tunnelling machine called a **mole** cuts through a mountain. Sharp **saws** on the front of the mole shave away the rocky cliff. Rock chips fall onto a moving belt which carries them out of the tunnel. As the mole pushes deeper into the mountain, workers put up concrete walls and a ceiling in the tunnel.

WORKER ON SEGMENT ERECTOR

SEGMENT CONVEYOR CRANE

CONVEYOR BELT

SLAG DUMPSTERS

mole

The tunnel-boring machine is named after an animal that is a fast digger. **Moles** make their homes underground in tunnels or burrows. They dig for worms and insects to eat.

On the other side of the mountain is another team of workers helping to build this tunnel. The two teams will tunnel toward each other and meet in the middle. The second team has reached a section of solid rock which is too hard for a tunnel-boring machine. They must use **explosives** to blast away the rock.

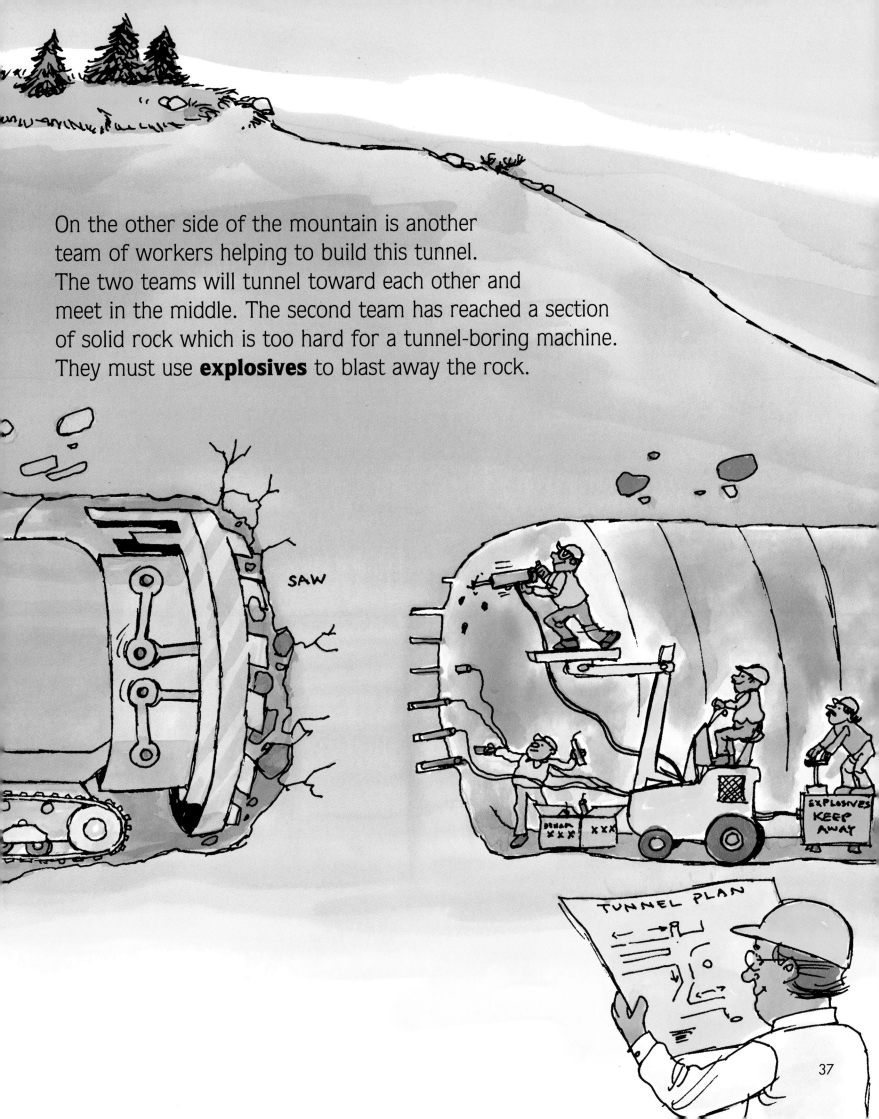

SAW

TUNNEL PLAN

EXPLOSIVES KEEP AWAY

Clifford Tells Time

At **seven o'clock** in the morning, Clifford peeks into Emily Elizabeth's window. "Hi, Clifford!" she calls. "Wait just a second." Clifford knows a second is the time it takes to blink his eyes.

Then Emily Elizabeth opens the window and gives Clifford a good-morning hug.

Clifford and Emily Elizabeth play in the park all morning. At **twelve noon** it's time for lunch. "Wait just a minute," says Emily Elizabeth. A minute is the time it takes to spread the picnic blanket and set out the lunch. Clifford can barely wait that long!

At **three o'clock** in the afternoon, Emily Elizabeth's friend Ashley comes over with her new puppy, Baby Henry. Emily Elizabeth and Ashley are going shopping. They want Clifford to babysit. "We'll be back in an hour," calls Emily Elizabeth. Clifford doesn't know how long an hour is, but just then Baby Henry lies down and closes his eyes.

At **four o'clock** the girls come back. Baby Henry wakes up. Now Clifford knows how long an hour is. An hour is the time it takes for Baby Henry's nap!

After their friends go home, Clifford and Emily Elizabeth play in the yard until dark. It's **seven o'clock** at night when Clifford has his dinner.

Clifford knows what time it is now. It's bedtime! By **seven-thirty** he is sound asleep.

Good night, Clifford!